Grandma's Alphabet

Marilyn A. Brownfield

Grandma's Alphabet

Copyright © 2025 Marilyn A. Brownfield

ISBN (Hardback): 979-8-89672-185-7
ISBN (Ebook): 979-8-89672-186-4

All rights reserved. No part of this book may be used or reproduced by any means, graphic, electronic, or mechanical, including photocopying, recording, taping or by information storage and retrieval system without the written permission of the author except in the case of brief quotations embodied in critical articles and reviews.

Because of the dynamic nature of the Internet, any web addresses or links contained in this book may have changed since publication and may no longer be valid. The views expressed in the work are solely those of the author and do not necessarily reflect the views of the publisher, and the publisher hereby disclaims any responsibility for them.

Printed in the United States of America.

PROMINENT
BOOKS
EDGE

5830 E 2nd St, Ste 7000 #9983
Casper, WY 82609
USA

Author's Message

I have always felt, that is extremely important for children to know the value of reading. I did not want my book to be one where the pages were turned very quickly, and then it was set aside somewhere. Imagination is a wonderful gift, and it allows a child to create happy images in their own minds. I hope that *Grandma's Alphabet* will be enjoyed and shared with siblings, parents, friends and grandparents.

Dedication

I dedicate this book to my children and grandchildren for all the love, happiness and precious memories they have filled my life with.

Allan the Alligator…
Ate a bowl of red Apples

Betty the **B**uffalo…

Blows up pink **B**alloons

Charlie the Caterpillar…

Crawls across the Carrots

Debbie the **D**ragonfly…
Drinks from sweet **D**aisies

Eddie the Elephant…
Eats toast with his Eggs

Francis the Frog…

Finds some new Friends

George the Giraffe...
Gobbles bunches of Grapes

Hannah the Horse...
Hurrys back to her Home

Izzie the **I**guana…

Invites us for **I**ce cream

Katie the Kangaroo...
Keeps flying paper Kites

Lawrence the Lion…
Likes cookies and Lollipops

Matilda the **M**onkey…

Makes bows for her **M**ittens

Nathan the **N**uthatch…
Needs to take a long **N**ap

Olivia the Octopus…

Opens a big jar of Olives

Patsy the **P**enguin…

Picks a bucket of **P**oppies

Quincy the **Q**uail…

Quickly stacks his **Q**uarters

Sammy the **S**eal…
Sings happy little **S**ongs

Teresa the **T**urtle…
Travels on a slow **T**rain

Ursela the **U**nicorn…

Uses a pretty **U**mbrella

Victor the **V**egetable…

Visits family on **V**acation

William the Worm...
Wiggles in a Watermelon

Xandra the **X**ylophone…
loves **X**oxoxo's and **X**oxoxo's

Yolanda the Yellowjacket…

Yes, she wants more Yogurt

Zachary the **Z**ebra…

Zigzags around the **Z**oo